THE LAND BARON'S SUN

The Story of Lý Loc and His Seven Wives

THE LAND BARON'S SUN

The Story of Lý Loc and His Seven Wives

Genaro Kỳ Lý Smith

University of Louisiana at Lafayette Press
2014

Cover Art: Will Turley

ISBN 13 (paper): 978-1-935754-35-0

University of Louisiana at Lafayette Press
P.O. Box 40831
Lafayette, LA 70504-0831
http://ulpress.org

Printed on acid-free paper.

Library of Congress Cataloging-in-Publication Data

Smith, Genaro Kỳ Lý, 1968-
  The land baron's sun : the story of Lý Loc and his seven wives
/ by Genaro Kỳ Lý Smith.
    pages cm
  ISBN 978-1-935754-35-0 (pbk. : acid-free paper)
  1. Vietnam--Poetry. I. Title.
  PS3619.M5859L36 2014
  811'.6--dc23
    2014007571

This book is dedicated to my wife, Robyn, our daughters Layla and Naomi, to my mother, Ngoc Thi, who left her family and her country behind to raise us in America, and to my father, Genera, for his guidance. This book is in memory of Lý Loc (1912-1992), my grandfather.

CONTENTS

III: What of My Wives and Children?

Epilogue

Acknowledgments

PROLOGUE

"Choosing not to engage in the story is the devastating part."

—Kenneth Robbins

In This House of Snails

In the core of this house,
six of Lý Loc's seven wives
sit around the family table.
With safety pins and needles,
they pluck snails from their spiraled homes,
dip their steaming curled bodies
in pepper and lemon paste and eat.
Satisfied with the way the snails turned out,
the wives speak of the garden's lush growth—
how they will have abundance
during the monsoon season—
and it is not long before their talks turn
to Lý Loc and how he has changed.

Mai (Monday) speaks of Loc's
mumbled confessions in his sleep
of sending manchild troops
to wither within their uniforms,
retract beneath brushes
and ground themselves in gullies
or in stretches of rich loam
along the riverbanks,
their innards spewed forth,
marking their own graves.

The youngest, Yên (Tuesday), feeds his hunger;
his tongue circles her nipple and areola
both clenched between his teeth, leaving marks
as he sates his taste from the abundance before him.

Viết (Wednesday) only sees the expanse of his back,
the sharp cliffs of his shoulder blades,
the raised ridges of his spine, the glen of each notch.
She learns the span of wasted time when he breathes.

Phương (Thursday) pries a snail
and cups its corpulent body on her tongue.
The first to bore Lý Loc a son,
she has produced thin, loose-limbed blue boys ever since,
boys whose necks lacked strength to hold up
their heads, their necks made malleable and soft
from prematurity.
One proved promising
when his belly swelled with first breath
and stayed swelled when the midwife
swathed him in silk in preparation for the ground.
Phương chews the snail's rubbery texture
to a softness she can swallow.

Ái (Friday) has no failures to report.
She tells the others as soon as he was done,
it was not long before he hardened and rose
again, feel the thrust of his hips driving into her.
The other wives lower their eyes
knowing that at age sixty-two
there is no second coming.

The wives extract more snails,
dip in paste, then chew
and nod at everything Ái says,
for they have heard Lý's snoring
resonating the walls washed early
from the moon of young evenings,
and those who come before or after her
know it is Friday.

Saturday, Van, plump Van,
only sings and blows a coronet,
and when he succumbs to slumber,
he cannot decipher the trill
of the woodwind or her singing;

says they rise and descend together,
waver in unison, feels the weight
of each note plummet him
from his place above the clouds
down to the tree lines,
feels rhythm's leverage ascend him
to heaven to grace the golden light of Christ.

Thanh, his first wife, is in another room, ingesting opium—
the smoke roils from her mouth and rises sluggishly.
The women's whispers become the constant,
hollow roar she heard as a young girl
when some boy picked up a half buried shell
on the shore of Cát Bà Island and shook it.
She told him to put it to his ear and listen.
"That is the sound of the sea: the winds, the waves,
the storms, the shifting clouds all contained
in one empty body. Snails sense sounds,"
she repeated what her mother had told her,
"and know there are places vacant
and untouched to accommodate growth."

Lying whorled in a fetal position,
Thanh ingests more opium.
Her mind working as slow as digestion,
she recalls watching the boy
and the trail he left in the wet sand
after adhering his parents' call
to come join them beneath the blue and white
umbrellas shading patrons who loaf in chaise lounges,
remembers the sound later that night
while awaiting sleep. She hoped
to see him again,
even replayed the way he turned red
when she asked if she could listen
and he placed the shell to her ear;

3

recalls the way he stammered
when he said he had to go.

They would see each other every summer—
he with only his widower father,
she looking for shells
different from the summer before—
until they matured into man and wife
and they were expecting their first.
He would imagine what their child looked like inside,
all coiled and constricted by the shape of the womb.
For months, he would place his ear to her stomach,
listen to rapid thrumming from within,
and he'd whisper promises—
his voice a muffled lull tremolo
echoing in his own ear—
of all the great things their child will do.

I

In Our House of Forever

View from the Veranda: An Elegy for Chan

Saigon fell last week on a day too gray for April—
columns of black smoke pyre and spiral upward,
informing Heaven of our failure in keeping the kingdom

intact. Saigon is still falling under the bludgeoning
weight of fire, and mortar rounds divot the city's surface
slow to scab and heal itself right again.

The Việt Cộng have begun the collection process going door to door
to bind and parade prisoners through the streets before loading them
into personnel carriers to be interrogated someplace else.

Today, as with yesterday, and the days before,
Chan, my Chinese servant and driver of forty years,
stands beside me on the veranda, a white cloth draped

over one poised arm, a decanter of Saki in the other
as we watch the abortion before us, watch the Việt Cộng
erase the cesarean line between North and South,

and my daughter, Vu-An, and her husband and son,
safe within the womb of American democracy, comes to mind.
I offered Chan the opportunity to leave with them,

to allow cataracts to milk over 'til blind in a country
that surrendered on a piece of paper and made sure to drown their helicopters
in the Gulf before leaving, but he refused, saying, "This is my home."

I continue to stare out over Saigon while my seven wives
and our remaining twenty children are still asleep
in sheets they will learn to launder for themselves,

and I am pleased they are not awake to see this,
but how they can sleep through the screams that siren the city,

or even worse, those same screams ceasing suddenly, escapes me.

The bottom part of the sky grows dense and dark
like Hell has latched onto Heaven's hem. Some time tomorrow,
Chan will rise before sun-up, dress in his white Nehru jacket

buttoned to the collar, his white slacks creased thin as documents.
He will make sure his loafers have a sheen that absorbs sunlight
before making the drive into the city and park the Citroën

outside Bến Thành Market, enter and select from buckets
of freshly cut carnations—a color per wife—pick through
the pyramidal displays of pears and apples and mangoes,

purple dragon fruits with gnarled, pointed scales,
bunches of longans and lichees, then make his way
to the beds of shaved ice to choose salt-preserved mackerels,

catfish, and tuna, some as big as small children. As with the past forty years,
he will bypass the young female vendors who plead too much,
whose fish are not as uniformly displayed on ice loosely packed

and buy from the old woman that has always been honest,
even admitting her catches were not from that morning.
Chan will secure a bottle of Saki; he will inventory his basket,

discover he has forgotten the incense sticks for my dead ancestors,
purchase plenty for the week, and then walk past the female vendors
who squint and even turn away when he steps outside into the white light.

THE ABDUCTION OF CHAN

I step outside Bến Thành Market
and soldiers wait by the Citroën,
erect and still as the rifles they brandish.
When they see me, their shoulders straighten
as authority and agenda dictate.
Instead of retrieving inside,
instead of feigning interest in the flower
and fruit vendors along the sidewalk
teeming with buyers bargaining prices,
I walk toward my master's car.

Dressed in all white—even the shoes—
I have to lower the brim of my pith helmet
to provide shade to ease the squinting,
ease the sudden attack on the eyes.
He is to be the third Chinese in a week,
and he is old enough to be my grandfather
who had long left this country and took solace
in Yunnan, the land south of the clouds.

One man opens the back door for me,
and before I climb inside,
another soldier takes my basket.
The others get in and we follow a personnel carrier
through the streets of spectators.
My hands rest on the leather upholstery
and I smooth my palms and realize
I am sitting where my master has sat for many years,
realize that I have never been a passenger,
and that the only time spent back here
was to wash and oil the back seat
until polished to a sheen.

I sit still and feel the indentation of my master,

and I am convinced I am him, revered by these men
who keep quiet during the drive the way I had been taught.

He is unbelievably calm for someone who must know his fate.
I want to ask him why he did not leave when the chance arose.
Even when I took the basket from his hand, he let go so easily
as though resigned to retire his life of servitude in that moment—
his whole life a servant readily relinquished like he had been waiting
to have the yoke removed from around his neck and shoulders.

We make it out to the countryside where the land is bare
of thatched huts, the ground untouched by plows and footsteps.
They walk me from the road through the tall grass,
and the one who took the basket from me carries it
by the crook of his arm as if finding the right spot for a picnic.

The man he works for is too wealthy: the load of his wants
weigh on my arm and I want to sling my rifle over one shoulder
and use both hands, but to do so would mean I am weak.

Relief comes as my brothers go through the basket,
dumping the carnations. One pockets incense sticks
while another grabs the bottle of Saki by the neck.
They pick their pears and pare mangoes,
and as they peel and eat the lichees and longans,
they debate when to cook the fish.
"Come," I tell the servant and motion my brothers to wait
while I walk the driver in white through this green ocean
of grass, and I wonder if he is the last Chinese I execute,
for I am to kill every one of them to prove myself
to the party, and to purify my half-breed status.

We enter a grove where the trees are wider than homes,
whose roots we have to scale until we come to a clearing,
and though cataracts make milky and murky my vision,
the sky is blue and cloudless as the one over Yunnan,

the province of my childhood.
And I know I am approaching my end,
knew this during the drive out of the city,
noting the kites flying over Saigon,
the strings tethered to the hands of faceless children
running in courtyards of apartment complexes and nearby parks.
Knew this while driving past *Saigon Notre-Dame Cathedral*,
its front doors and stained-glass windows boarded up
by men in black pajamas.
Sitting in the backseat of my master's car,
St. Gabriel came to mind: *when the time nears,*
a prominent memory from childhood will appear.

Red and yellow kites come into view now,
stationed high and unmoving; the butterflies with painted eyes,
the papered dragons with long ribbon-adorned tails gauge wind and altitude,
and I am seven again, the last year I was allowed to be a boy
before I became a servant.

He keeps looking up at the sky, never at the ground
for sure footing. He unbuttons his Nehru jacket,
lets it slide off his arms, and the grass is so tall, so sturdy,
the jacket never touches ground. He tosses aside the cap,
unbuttons his shirt, and it is like watching a ghost
come apart a wisp at a time. He slips off his loafers,
unzips his trousers, and I slow down, look over my shoulders
at the wall of thick banyan trees to see if anyone is watching,
watching something queer unfolding before me.

I raise my rifle, bark a harsh, "Hey! Hey!,"
but he keeps undressing until he is nude,
and the sun makes light of a map of thin purple veins
coursing the surface of his old skin. He kneels facing China,
and I expect him then to plead like the others
who shook their praying fists at me,
bargaining to my Chinese half,

but the chauffeur remains on his knees,
praying about walking through some valley
with a shadow named Death.

A white robe descends from the sky,
and little angels dress me and fashion a rope
around my waist, and still, two more angels alight
with something gold and blinding in their hands,
and they fit it upon my head,
my crown ornamented with rubies
and sapphires and emeralds.

St. Gabriel places the horn to his lips and blows,
and there is new music from just one note—
loud and booming, and the obliteration of the din
that is my beloved Vietnam is now a ringing
echoing throughout every bone,
muscles and tendons fevered taut,
each tooth loosened from its root,
the nerve plucked like chords,
one note rifling through this pasture
and careening over mountains
before ascending to a deafening fanfare
announcing my arrival into His kingdom.

They are where I left them, sated by what the basket had to offer,
and I motion for my brothers to go.
I sit in the back of the Citroën, wanting to tell the others
how calm he remained throughout it all,
even angry at my brothers for not asking if I had any trouble;
did he whimper while begging for his life.
They do not know that I asked the chauffeur
if he had any last requests, anyone I should notify?
He said he wanted to watch the kites
welcome his departure from this world.
As we head home, I spot specks afloat in the sky above Saigon.

Some are stationary, some move in circles, and for a moment
I thought the servant's God granted him his wish,
for the kites are so high that I imagine boys tying spools
and spools of string together in hopes of having their kites get lost
in some corner of Heaven for the chauffeur to find.

I imagine when the wind dies
or picks up suddenly, snagging the strings out of their hands,
the children will run to catch them,
run in dizzying patterns
trying to anticipate where they will land.

The Collection Process

When they came, they discovered a bevy of wives
sitting at a table, our husband eating dinner
when they ordered him to stand,
but Lý Loc remained seated,
determined to finish his meal.
There came the thrush of parted chairs,
a siren of wives' screams,
some lodged in their throats
from ever completing alarm.

They scoffed at our husband,
pointed their pistols at his penis,
wondering how could he have pleased us.
They dropped his pants
and stared at what wrinkled between his legs;
they even gauged each wife,
then back between his legs,
and then at each of us again
before anger surged through Lý Loc
and he blinded the nearest
with his pair of chopsticks,
backhanded the next, began beating back another
before a barrage of them bludgeoned
and bled him into submission on all fours.
We cowered in one corner,
the bowls of rice disturbed, the Saki spilled,
fowl and fish fell to the floor.

They raised him by his arms and led him outside,
and we congregated at the window.
Never had I seen him that old, that stooped,
that unstable on his feet that two men had to assist him
inside the crammed personnel carrier.
The doors closed to what would be the last time

I ever saw my husband—our husband—
the starched white collar of his shirt
stained from head wounds,
the reverence shown by the others
who moved over to make room.

OUR DAILY BREAD

Lý Loc's first week serving in a reeducation camp

It's the same rhetoric every morning—
wake before the sun, clothe ourselves,
file outside before our barracks
and listen to the trees instruct us
on how to be Uncle Hồ's children;
that our minds are not our own but Vietnam's
and we must show our cause
by taking up the sickles and hoes
and march into the fields.
I remember my first morning waking up
in the *cooperatives*, thinking God, who called us
from the trees, spoke Vietnamese
and that His son spoke it too,
not Aramaic, not Hebrew, nor Latin or even French.

That first day working sixteen hours in the fields
made me feel like one of His banished sons,
for the air were hands that held us under,
and we had to rear our heads and shoulders
in protest of His callous palms
as we slew stalks from the earth,
rolled them into bundles to rend grains free
from their sheaths against bamboo mats
and collected His bountiful harvest with our small hands.
He moved us like oxen and His invisible yoke,
heavy on our shoulders, yanked us up by our frayed collars
whenever we staggered or fell to our knees.
Still, His voice broadcasted from the trees
discouraging us from the weight of thinking.

I thought of the guards that day not as brothers
as they insisted we called them, and not as Uncle Hồ's children,
but God's ordained bishops and cardinals and appointed popes

16

brandishing Russian AK47s and M16s they had pilfered from dead GIs—
leaving them unarmed and defenseless in the afterlife—
drilling catechism to the back of our heads
whenever we backslide, or they marked our bodies
with a number of rosaries for sins to be forgiven.
At the end of the day, they always remembered the addle-minded,
the weak who failed to harness and shoulder their load,
the ones who wilted brown beneath the sun;
they always remembered those whose tongues betrayed them
and graced the gliding syllables of French or the abrupt stops required
of English or hummed hymns to Christ:
they were the ones whose names were called from His roll book
to be summoned forth from the barracks before mealtime
and escorted by minions to be sacrificed in the fields.

And we thank God for having called the others before us;
those whose offerings proved to be as insufficient as Cain's;
we thank God their blood would suffice for the time being
and I recall that first day they let us sit a spell in the shade,
recall my back against one of the trunks
and I felt a wire vine its way up the tree
to a set of speakers nestled among the coconuts.
During our respite, we continued to hear Him,
the rise and fall, the weighted stress on certain syllables
that lulled our hearts and breathing to a calm.
That calm was not there after the names had stopped being called.
After the fields crackled with gunshot we were allowed
to eat and sleep, and that first night when I laid my head to rest,
I knew that come next day, in order to silence the summoning of names
to be sacrificed in the fields, I was going to take my sickle
and sever God's vocal cords.

REPLETION

Jaws do not align right when broken,
yet bones graft and heal erect
to sturdiness they once held.
The raised red welts swell
beyond obtaining the textured health of perfect white skin.
The knuckles gnarl from swinging hoes,
picks, and sickles under the weight
of saturated days we heft on our backs and shoulders,
and our heads bear the weight of the sun's crown.

We travel the length of the field and feel the puss boil,
sweat stains and seeps inside open wounds we incurred
from mishandling blades, from splinters swelling
and growing black underneath skin,
slashes and cuts we accrued
from working around Red Dragon grass.
With machetes strapped around waists,
gun belts tight around their chafed necks
and rifles brandished like insults,
Uncle Hồ's children gauge our progress.

During the long and arduous hours in the rice fields,
I can only think of my wives in the kitchen
cooking cubes of caramelized, glazed pork,
stir-frying morning glories till glistening,
broiling mackerels to darken their already brown meat,
dipping rice papers and setting them on the table
to lie limp until rolled with shrimps, noodles, cucumbers,
chives, lettuce, and sprouts into tight white bundles.
I think of *nước mắm* speckled with pale pepper seeds,
steamed snails, of rice passed around the table I once headed,
mouths full from the abundance before them,
their arms reaching across the table for plenty,
and I wield this scythe to fell rice for a *cooperative*
whose objective is to teach me of my prior life of avarice.

18

As the day's labor hardens my muscles,
as my raging welts await the comfort of sleep,
I tilt my head back, maneuver undercooked rice
with swollen fingers to allow the grains
to slide down my throat,
bitter by my wives' simple ability to chew.

DREAMING OF YÊN

The sky is an endless field of flesh, soft and light,
groaning and burning underneath me, my youngest wife:
I was between you, then behind you,
and I dirtied what I tried to keep so white,
so clean in our house of forever.

I lie awake now, erect, trying to make real this dream,
or at least prolong it, so I touch myself.
Though the air is sticky and foul,
I surrender to the dream and erupt white and thick,
the warmth flowing down the back of my knuckles.
I let out a moan, knowing the men cannot hear me
above the cicadas and frogs and crickets creating a cacophony.

How I miss the slow slathered fucks of our mornings,
the sluggish wet ways we moved, twining arms and legs
as we joined at the hips and writhed beneath sheets,
behind the translucent veil of our canopy bed.
I heard the government parceled my property to other men,
and I imagine your new husband struck dumb upon seeing you
the way I was on our wedding night—the other wives vanquished from the house.
You sat waiting behind the mosquito netting fine as spider's silk,
thin-limbed with legs folded within yourself, arms collapsed around them.

I caressed and held the weight of your washed hair heavy as ropes
before fumbling with the clasps of your *áo dài.*
I parted the panels and peeled away the gown to expose your skin.
The contrast of your breasts—clean of blemish, absent of blushing—
cupped in my veinal, bony hands made me aware of my age.
But the supple, pointed rupture of your nipples, the warmth rising from your flesh
made me feel youthful again as you supplied my hunger, my thirst by lying back
and parting your legs. Though your thighs against my ears muffled
the sounds of the night—the cicadas screeching, the crickets chirping, the frogs croaking,
a distant city lit and bombarded and buried beneath mortar rounds—
I could not tell if the floor shook, or if it was my heart thundering,
or simply your small body, tensed and trembling on my tongue.

GRASPING

Nguyễn, our overseer, wakes with ease like every morning
as we remain stilled by the weight of wet air pressing us
down. Prying skin and spine from beds of split reeds,

each man rises and turns toward Nguyễn, silhouetted and framed
in the glassless window of our barracks. Though he wears
a long-sleeve shirt, one is empty and pinned at the shoulder

we have seen where the doctor pruned the stump
for perfect healing while he washed at the end of long days
spent harvesting Heaven's crop of rice and cane.

His missing arm reminds us of beds we once inhabited,
of sheets warmed by arms and legs entwined,
the sounds of our wives' dreams patterned by their breathing,

the comfort of their hearts pulsing in our palms
when placed against their chest during rest,
the guarantee that we would never part from them.

Our welts are the alarm clocks of our bodies.
The soreness in our muscles crescendo with a siren's shrill
reminding us of healings that will never happen.

As each man yawns while dressing, Nguyễn continues to wait the dawn—
darkness turns dim, and the stars pale in their promise
of appearing another night to lull us to sleep.

Fully dressed, we file outside to God's daily rhetoric,
and we wonder if it rained last night. It must have, for a rainbow
comes down from beyond the horizon of trees like some miracle

and we wish the colors are something tangible, something
we can grasp, but it is a prism of light and air and water,

a reminder of the evening's rain we all missed, a façade

as empty as unanswered prayers. We take up our sickles and sacks
and march into the fields where God's abundance awaits us to fell His crops,
but we are distracted by the rainbow, its girth the size of a district.

Though we are to keep our heads down while working,
Nguyễn stops to stare at the rainbow; perhaps he is remembering
a time when he was able to climb trees with the other boys,

or help his father reel in lines and nets to fill the creel, then row ashore
when they had enough to feed the family; we wonder if his wife loved him
even more when he came home, or did she look at the floor every time

she spoke to him, or did she sleep away from the center of the bed.
We keep working while Nguyễn is most likely recalling his childhood
and the many times he walked toward a rainbow, as so many of us had,

thinking it was only a field away, thinking, *Just on the other side of those trees,*
just on the other side of the those trees and I can be in its glow,
touch it even and tell the other children of my village what I was able to do.

RAISE THE DAY, LOWER THE NIGHT

We will the day to rise,
summon the sun
to lift the weight of its heat,
lift the weight of its rays
that covet our faces,
weld the clothes to our skin,
rise so that our lungs
are reminded of apparitions
between breathing and suffocation.

So many of us have wanted
to lay down our labor,
remove our sun hats and sandals,
strip off our clothes
and lie on our backs as an offering,
a prayer to the sun
to die down its daily time
and sacrifice itself to darkness,
part the day's curtains,
lower the black velvet backdrop
with its moon and stars veiled by shifting clouds.
Let the lack of light cool our limbs
as we lie there in the mud
among the stalks and crickets;
feel Your heat rise from us,
take back what You gave all day
and leave us what we willed for
when we tried to latch ourselves
to each other's shadow for shade
when You provided none for us.

II
THE LAND SOUTH OF THE CLOUDS

VACATION

North Vietnam, 1918

I.

I met the back of God's hand once
as a boy of eight, long before Hồ Chí Minh thought
of overthrowing the French.
My father drove us from Hanoi
to vacation on Cát Bà Island,
and I remember that morning
still veiled in fog, dense and milky as pearls:
the rubber trees waded through their morning
while awakened workers carved lines
along their bark until white sap coursed and bled
into pails the farmers satcheled against tree trunks.

Ahead, the boulders rose above the fog,
the coastline blurred to where the land divorced itself
from the South China Sea. I remember
it took two hours to get to Hạ Long Bay
to board a boat for Cát Bà Island.
I remember the slowness of my father's driving,
the ivory cigarette filter poised between his lips,
my mother reading *La Vie* magazine to take her mind off
what grew inside her thinned her outside.

And still the fog drowned the road
that rose and fell beneath us,
the boulders loomed as big as planes,
as big as I imagined God's knuckles,
and we were driving over the back of God's hand,
entering heaven the back way.
It felt like cheating,
like we would get caught,
and His knuckles would form fists

27

to shake us free of Him. Coming off the last knuckle,
we arrived at a wharf of boats.
The boatman and his crew crowded our car
to cart our luggage onto the boat,
and father unfurled *đồngs* to tip the crew
and the boatman's fee to pilot us past the horizon of rocks.

II.

On Cát Bà Island, the sun fails to burn off
the layer of an overcast day,
and Mother's first afternoon is spent
on the beach beneath blue and white umbrellas
as she stares at that horizon of rocks:
God's spine, she once said. The boat pilot who ferried us through
to Cát Bà had known every notch of His column,
navigated each bone of His spine since childhood
to bring the forlorn and faithful to Heaven,
to bring us to a beach lined with chaise lounges
and umbrellas and servants waited on patrons.
Mother reposed in her chair and stared
at God's rough vertebrae from behind her sunglasses,
underneath her sun hat, as Father read and smoked.
He perused Mother between turning pages,
trying to remember how she was before the diagnosis.

At eight years old, I believed God existed as something
small and black inside her, that He grew, vined and knotted,
cleaved and pooled purple at the surface to show
where He had racked her white skin to ruin.
God had mapped the very landscape of her pain,
mapped the locations the French doctors had said
they could cut and singe, scoop and discard
in hopes of healing her. But no promise of mercury
or any amount of ether could change her mind.

28

She stood up, dropped the hat and the sunglasses,
announced that it was too hot and walked toward the water.
She walked past little children sculpting mounds,
past the ones wading and kicking in the water,
past the older ones floating on their backs
until she was swallowed by the vast expanse of green.

Father followed and stood ashore, one hand over his brows
as flat, foamless waves encircled his ankles.
Mother kept paddling out to where it seemed the blue sky
cleaved the green South China Sea.
He called out to her, told her she had gone too far,
and she stopped and faced us, and though she was far away,
she was smiling with God's spine behind her,
His unseen hardened knuckles still clenched along the mainland
as she dunked herself, bathing in His golden cure-all.

III.

We came home a week later after days of swimming,
of flying kites and fishing, of eating rice,
caramelized pork, stir-fried morning glories,
braised shrimp and steamed snails,
mackerels wrapped in paper and cooked in pits.
And always Father had insisted Mother
should eat more, for we never knew *when*.

With one arm over Father's shoulder, her other resting
on mine, we helped her work her way upstairs
to the room she had known since marriage
when she, the new bride and wife, slept the first night
close to the bed's edge, uncertain what was to take place.
We placed her in the bed she had grown tired of
from daily rests, tired of whispered prayers
from nurses in white, tired of their hanging crosses
and black rosary beads hovering over her,

tired of watching the day
start off dark, dim, bright, dim, and dark again
all from her bed. So she slept for three days
upon our return, and never once
did she go outside for sun or drizzle,
for birds or thick bloomed flowers.

She just slept and slept, until she slept herself
in the ground where God folded His fingers over her
and held Mother in the soft flesh of His palm.

THE LAND BARON'S SUN
Vinh Long, South Vietnam, 1919

Months after Mother's death,
after months of mourning her,
Father takes me along to survey the land.
"One day, this will all belong to you,"
he says, gesturing out the car window
at the rice fields slewed by harvesters,
the acres of rubber trees with trunks scarred
where workers drained them of sap into pails
to be processed in mills.

His hand remains outside the car
as though gauging his speed
as we pass the sugarcane fields.
Still, his hand is poised
when passing the mango, coconut,
and banana groves and more rice fields.
The sun is rising over the horizon,
and I am waiting for the moment
when both hands are on the steering wheel
marking an invisible line of land
he no longer owns.

"From now on, you will come with me
so I can show you how things are done
for when I am gone."

We come to a pear orchard,
the fruits round and pale
and not yet ripe with freckles.
I realize as he drives past,
the women and men stop their labor
to lean their picks and scythes against their legs
and remove their sun hats to bow.

Even those high up the ladders
or along the limbs filling sacks cease.
A wave of workers' heads fall forward
as Father nears.

He stops the car and I follow him
into a makeshift village.
"I must tend to the rent," Father tells me.
"Stay out here. Play with the others,"
he motions to the children running around the village of huts,
around the pump well,
beneath the rows of sheets and shirts stretched
on clotheslines fashioned between trees,
kicking and chasing a ball with sticks in hands.
I wait until Father approaches one of the huts
and enters without knocking and closes the door behind him
before joining the other children behind the row of huts,
and they are all on their knees,
parting fronds to peek inside the one my father entered.
I want to ask them what they are doing,
but one looks over at me, and without a word,
he moves over and continues to peer inside
a place of moaning and hoarse breathing.
I kneel and look inside and air is caught in my throat,
for Father, fully clothed, struggles on top of a woman.
I do not know the motions they make with their bodies,
but I am held still and breathing through my mouth
while we watch the woman move to Father's rhythm.
Her bare legs angle to the sides, her brown arms wrap
around his neck and shoulders.
Her head is turned to one side, her eyes closed
as she mumbles a mantra we do not understand.

The heat from their laboring smells,
and the early morning warmth bears down on me
as Father's breathing becomes harsher.

He buries his face between her neck and shoulder
to muffle a moan followed by a whimper,
and all movement between them stop
and they become limp.
They lay that way, still, and breathing before
he stands up, and she remains on the floor,
hands over her chest made flat by gravity.
Without a word from either one, Father leaves,
and we scurry to our feet.
The boys resume their play
filling the morning with laughter and rising dust.
Father calls for me, and I come from around the huts,
and he is different:
his face is flushed and damp
like it will never return to its pale stature, his eyes aflame,
and because he wears a silk robe buttoned to the neck,
I can see his chest swell with each breath.

As we leave the village of huts,
the children swirl about the place
chasing the ball lost between their legs
and their laughter and flailing limbs
kick up a storm of dust that linger
among the trees, coating the pears.
Father takes out his neckerchief
and dabs at his forehead,
at his neck, the area above his lips.
He stares down the road,
facing the sun leveled with the horizon.
I can only make out Father's silhouette:
with hands on hips, he assesses
all the land and people he owns
before dropping his arms to walk towards the sun
to tend to something bigger than all of us.
I stand rooted as I wait to witness
what I have overheard our servants say he did:

make the sun come down
and show its crown while Father collects
what it owes him.

THE PORTRAITIST

Lý Loc, 15, experiences his first love with a French art instructor's daughter, Michelle Jolibois, 17, who attends Lê Hồng Phong, a school for gifted French students. Only a select few Vietnamese are allowed admission, those of royalty or whose fathers are high-ranking officials. Michelle Jolibois is commissioned by Lý Loc's father to paint a family portrait. Saigon, 1925.

Mon sacré bleu!*
I have never seen
a Vietnamese boy as tall as he,
taller than my father even,
as he enters the study in full regalia
to take his place with his family:
his dark blue tunic is buttoned
to a collar starched stiff
to hold his face in place;
his cuffs cover the knobs of his wrists;
the epaulettes gleam golden
in natural light.

I stand behind the easel,
studying each member,
but my eyes always go to him,
to his closely cropped hair
stiff as new paint bristles,
his slender jaw crafted
toward a clean-cleft chin.

I want to erase his family members
who pose old and white,
stand poised with thin, stiff lips,
and only paint him,
but my canvas, long stretched and nailed
to the wooden frame,

_____
* My heavens!

35

is marred by what I can fit
onto this square piece.

What I want instead is us
in a sampan on the Mekong,
passing beneath ships
whose holds do not contain gold
and spice and silk, or fish
large enough to swallow small children,
but nets heavy with a harvest of hearts
of men who have died
throughout the centuries
while crossing oceans
in search of their other halves.

I grip the charcoal,
sketch each member onto my canvas,
eager for the moment
I mix paint to color him
within my borders,
render a shade of blue
I had seen only once before
taking residency here.
For now, he emerges
prominent in coal,
his family members mere
dreary shadows of gray
in his light.

Communion

Michelle Jolibois made a return visit to capture on canvas a shade of blue true to Lý Loc.

You did not protest when Chan led you into the study,
angled the door-length jalousies to cast light upwards
as if the sun shone from the ground, nor when he joined

the French doors and slid the bolt inside the tight niche
made swollen by summer heat, then turned the knob
forcing locked the doors. Alone, we labored at the clasps

and straps and buttons to unclothe ourselves.
Though we stood among the shelved leather-bound books
with spines embossed with glossy, gold lettering,

though surrounded by the jade figurines of Buddha
of various sizes, statued-monks, lacquered urns taller than us,
oracle bones and mammoth tusks unearthed in China,

your nude body became my treasured grail—
pail and freckled, bone-thin around the ribs and hips.
Our breathing settled from the promise of touching,

at the prospect of our mouths on each other. Today,
I am on my knees collecting strands of your brown hair
where we lay, a communicant going through the rosary.

I rely on thoughts of you to nourish the fasting periods.
Deprived of my taste for you, I am unable to sleep,
and so I pace this room housing your absence, your hair

a reminder of our sinning in my father's house.
For the past days, you move across the firmament
of my waking hours filled with visions of a heaven

adorned with columns and courtyards with fountains affixed
with maidens, martyrs, cherubs, and saints sculpted
in moments of salvation. You came to me

with your liturgy of lines, your palette of colors,
charcoal and brushes you wield like scepters you pass
over your canvas perched on your three-legged altar

upholding a faith I want to embrace, catechism I answer
each night, a name I whisper as soft as prayer,
a consecrated host dissolving on my tongue.

Where God Sleeps: The Genesis of Michelle Jolibois' Sexual Awakening

I.

Father has been sketching and painting landscapes of Italy,
and though we stopped in Torino so he could sketch the *Apennines*,
even visited the *Cathedral of Saint John the Baptist* and stood in awe
before the glass entombment of Jesus' shroud; though we touched
one foot of *The David* at The Ufizi in Fiorenza, it grew old:
embarking and unloading at every village, every city these past four months.

Often, Cousin Sophia and I toured the villages or cities,
strolled the marketplaces and frequented the cafes,
or picnicked somewhere and read books
while Father set his easel on leveled surfaces with his valise of paints
and brushes and charcoal displayed. He would squint behind bifocals
as he stood erect in pin-striped slacks and matching vest,
his dress shirt buttoned to his neck,
the sleeves rolled up to his elbows.
He would squint against the light to capture God's abundant gifts:
a field of lavender stretching the length of the horizon
interrupted by a grove of trees; coifed farmers bent double
while harvesting rows of grapes and tomatoes; the monasteries perched
in the hillsides, castles long abandoned and kept chaste;
a vertical, leaning tower he painted in a day,
afraid it might fall before he was through.

Four months' journey, and we wind up in Sorrento,
our luggage and chests unloaded by porters
as dark as the sun-scorched, salt-sprayed cliff sides.
No sooner than we check into a villa does Father
walk Sorrento, the narrow avenues that lead to dead ends,
or come out onto delightful courtyards, and he walked and walked—
certain he was trying to forget Mother, or at least make grieving bearable—
until he sees *Cattedrale dei Santi Filippo e Giacomo,* naked and white,

tucked between two buildings, sees men huddled at the base,
huddled like worshippers weeping at the feet of a bleeding Jesus,
huddled as they size and saw marble slabs before lifting them
to clothe the façade of their place of devotion.
Without invitation, without their ever asking, Father takes off his jacket,
drops it on the ground, rolls up his sleeves, and takes part
with the locals in the resurrection of marble tiles,
preserving what they find most sacred and beautiful.

*

Father returns to our villa, clothes covered with marble dust,
to a table of wine, and next to it, a telegram he opens with apprehension:

Paris October 14 1924

Mon ami Jolibois I hope you are doing well STOP *I hope my friend that Italy
suits you in your time of need* STOP *that this respite will help soften the agony
of your loss* STOP *Once again I want to express just how sorry I am* STOP
*Melinda was and will forever be the wonderful woman I have always admired
and adored* STOP *Having said that I wish to impart some great news which
concerns you and I think your daughter Michelle will be most pleased as well*
STOP *Société des lettres sciences et arts de Paris has voted unanimously to
have you head the art school at Lê Hồng Phong in Saigon* STOP *I believe this
new post is what is needed* STOP *Who knows Marc perhaps you will meet
someone new once you acquaint yourself with the parents and family friends of
those who have lived in Cochin china for many years* STOP *Perhaps this lotus
will make you love again* STOP *to seek comfort in a woman's embrace* STOP
to appreciate life once again STOP *I await your reply* STOP *Take care my
good friend* STOP

Sincerely
President Alexandre Millerand FULL STOP

II.

Father busily works *Cattedrale dei Santi Filippo e Giacomo*
from morning till dusk, hands hardened and calloused from handling
freshly cut marble. At nights he gathers with other local artists

to drink wine, have their fill of grapes and cheeses
and vinegar-soaked sardines and tomatoes.
Cousin Sophia and I are free to roam around

the coastal boardwalk of Sorrento during the day,
fond over by men vulgar enough to publically pucker at us
and fill the air with kisses, or they stretch their syllables

more than required to simulate the length of how long
they want to love us. How good they can be to us.
I lower my head to let loose hair hide my blushing.

One day while sunbathing, Sophia and I attract the attention
of two men. Their talks cease by blushing from what she told them:
*Voi uomini italiani sono solo chiacchiere. Proprio come il tuo pene.**

Her profanity made them come over to lounge around the borders
of our blankets, wary of how close they are allowed to come.
Their elbows sink into the sand from the weight of their apologies,

and for the next three days, they make up for it by treating us
to coffee or *gelato* at cafes they can afford, *tortellini* and wine
from a restaurant with a view of Vesuvius, erect but dormant;

take us to *Cuomo's* shop to watch artisans shape wood into music
and cigar boxes, furniture, card tables and chess boards,
the wooden blocks they chisel into rooks and kings and queens

and pawns, castle their bishops fit for knights;
the grandfather clocks and other time pieces
meant to adorn foyers and hallways, or centerpieces in dens,

carved and sanded, then fondled over for the right curvature
or the right sharpness of corners; they run thumbs to detect any nicks
and depressions and hone as perfectly as God would see fit

---

*You Italian men are only small talk. Just like your penises.

to house in His home before applying shellac to capture the sheen of His light.
By day three, Cousin Sophia wants to be taken to His home
inside the Blue Grotto—the base of *Isle di Capri*—

the mouth of God where Tiberius had a procession of boats
brought inside with women and corpulent tomatoes and grapes,
roasted pigs on silver platters and chalices filled with wine

for gluttonous days of eating, drinking, and orgies. Cousin Sophia and I
have overheard my father's colleagues relate stories of when youth
and lust journeyed their pliable bodies to desecrate God's bed,

to offer up the parts of themselves they wished to ruin,
a place where God still sleeps. "We are gentlemen," one says.
In perfect Italian, Cousin Sophia says, "*Non vogliamo gentiluomini.*"*

III.

The hired oarsman works a rhythm while wresting with the waves.
At the mouth of Grotto, God yawns blue and thirsty, each wave
a lap of His tongue reminiscent of Tiberius' unquenchable thirst

for wine and food, for women and boys, and the men smile
with the same prospect of claiming. The glow from within God's mouth
beacons each heartbeat to succumb, but as the oarsman works

and winds his way toward the mouth, over God's lapping tongue
that drinks us in, my heart races once inside, and the roof of God's mouth
is lit blue by sunlight rising from His lime-bed at the ocean's floor.

With the boat anchored, the oarsman produces paper and tobacco.
The men doff their caps and shirts, step out of their trousers, and our eyes go
to the triangular matts of hair from which their eagerness protrudes.

They dive in and scissor their arms and legs, their brown bodies

---

*"We don't want gentlemen."

aglow in God's favored hue. Cousin Sophia stands up
much to the indifference of the oarsman who puffs on his cigarette;

she unties the broad straps from around her neck and steps out of the one-piece,
exposing breasts too big for her age, a body curved like a grown woman's,
and the men and I stare at what gifts God granted her.

I undress and dive in, hoping not to have them stare too long
at my slim form, lack of hips, hoping he is not disappointed by breasts
that can be swallowed whole even by my own hands.

His smile never wavers as he leads me to a rock the size of God's molar:
he cups one breast, his mouth around the other, his other hand works
toward a buttock, and then he plunges his tongue inside my mouth

and I feel his engorged warm self between me and I grip his shoulders
and neck as he writhes a rhythm inside me, the heat from our bodies
fever. Our panting and grunting join Cousin Sophia's languorous moans

and with each thrust, he swells and rises, and in rising he rainbows a rhythm
within me. Our beating hearts, our panting and grunting overcome
the recurring sound of the waves gnashing against the molars and cusped

upon which we lay supine like lovers forever captured in murals,
our ecstasy echoing before escaping God's gaping mouth to fall upon the ears
of fishermen who row out to sea, lonesome for their wives awaiting their return.

ERRAND BOYS

I know the day's schedule before Lý Loc rises,
know to cart the easel, charcoal, and tubes of colors
and paint brushes, or to carry leather-bound books
about lust-filled lovers;

know to have his rackets properly stringed,
that the day's weather warrants a white sweater vest
while playing tennis or just a long sleeve shirt
he may roll up to the elbows.

The Moroccans who chauffeur their masters' children
are not allowed on the courtyards or in the classrooms,
their skin as dark as the colored regions of African maps,
their tightly tucked turbans kept intact

with bejeweled stickpins deemed too threatening to the school's image.
And so, I am the only one who retrieves a towel for my master
so that he may wipe his hands and wrists, his brow
and neck of sweat in between sets.

The French students stare, for Lý Loc is the only one
who has an attendant to go with him to every class,
who sits in the corner, silent and attentive to the lectures and lessons.
I notice the way the girls look at him

as he sits erect at his desk, his head still as he conjugates Latin
and French verbs, learns which consonants remain silent when reciting
aloud. The girls in stiff-collared blouses, their pleated skirts
that come close to their ankle-socks,

hair ribboned low enough to hide their napes watch him
at lunchtime maneuver chopsticks, the quiet sips of tea,
but they do not know he is this meticulous, this methodical
and patient with the women

44

back home in Vinh Long where we return at the end of each school term
to collect the rent; the number of times I have waited outside the huts
and quieted my breathing to listen to the women's moans turn slowly
in their throats. He works a rhythm

to prolong his stay, delay their sighing, works a motion unfamiliar
to them having been accustomed to the rough handling of farmers
whose movements are synonymous with the plowing of fields,
the thrashing of crop,

the gutting and portioning of livestock and fowl. He is his father,
who left acres for his son's personal plundering. When we return to Saigon,
to Lê Hồng Phong, the French girls stand in circles and wonder
how Lý Loc spent his respite.

The dutiful servant that I am remains quiet while the Moroccans
in crisp white uniforms gather at the parade of parked Phantoms,
relieved of their brood to smoke Turkish cigarettes and drink tea
they buy from female peddlers

who make their way up and down sidewalks shouldering poles
with baskets hanging from both ends. The Moroccans share stories
of their masters falling asleep in the laps of Vietnamese maids
who caressed their heads behind bamboo

and silk screens, share stories of which boy has an affinity for their maids.
The first day of the new term in art class, I part the legs of my master's easel,
and though Michelle Jolibois wears a long dress, she stands with legs parted,
the other girls remember to scissor theirs closed.

Moth Songs

I want to know the names
of moths as big as bats,

their wings fluttering
with the panicky speed

of hummingbirds' heartbeats,
but like smaller moths

we are accustomed to,
they fly into walls,

screened verandas, the nettings around beds,
bat themselves against lit lanterns

to release dust and soot
from their fine gossamer wings

inlaid with plumage as colorful as a bird's,
their bodies pregnant with the ripeness of life.

I have heard certain moths cannot be touched,
their silk-dust wings having human imprints

mark their enabling us to come too close to them,
and they are grounded forever,

like heaven having lost its angels
and cherubs due to sinning.

Like Dante's Francesca and Paola entwined,
their flesh meld together by hell's forever fire.

This is how my days are spent
as I watch white rice brown in black skillets,

or I walk into doors before I think
to open them because I am always moving towards you,

certain of your name, certain of the source
of light that consumes me at night.

HER THOUSAND LOVERS

Mademoiselle Jolibois is like the moths
flitting from one classmate

to the next, Chan tells me, to swap
words of pollen and pulp,

to exchange sap and nectar
from their cheeks and lips

as she weaves and circles
desks and chairs, potted palms and *mai* trees

in the courtyard, brushes past
the creased legs and pleated skirts

to take in everyone in her arms.
But she was a spider in another life—

an eight-legged arachnid
who spent hours in moonlight

crocheting webs, not beneath wooden eaves,
or Russian Olive branches; nor between bamboo

shoots and sickly sweet saffron,
but outside the windows of boys who dreamt

of their first, dreamt of their own girth
and length capable of emoting moans

from the mouths of girls who fought to dislodge
surprise caught in their throats.

It is there, outside their windows she awaits
each night in centers she created.

Legs outstretched and stilled,
she is silenced by shrieking cicadas,

the crickets' celloing legs, the grasshoppers' harps,
the palmettos tromboning, and the staccato buzz

of mosquitoes and gnats who fly into
the designed mesh of fine, thin illumined silk

only to flap in tremulous states of excitement
as she races to clothe them

in threads of hunger and feeding,
close her legs and arms around them

until their fluttering settles
to a calmness they think is home.

INTERMISSION

"Beautiful are the feet of messengers who bring good news."
—Romans 10:15

PROVIDENCE

At St. Francis Xavier, November 2, 1963

Not even President Diệm
could convince air to come into his lungs,
nor could he writhe his hands free of ropes,

or engineer his skull and flesh, the bones
that structured and held his frame in place,
to harden and deflect bullets

that entered and violated what was most sacred,
only to succumb to a heap
in the back of an armored personnel carrier.

I wondered what he thought as he and his brother,
Nhu—haggard after a sleepless night
of fleeing from a palace of tall white columns

and marbled floors, of long dinner tables
with empty straight-backed chairs
and courtyards of ponds where water caressed

smooth-shelled rocks constructed into tiny falls,
ponds adorned with sharp-billed Birds of Paradise
with tufts of orange and blue—crossed

St. Francis Xavier's shaded courtyard and entered
the church after Mass had celebrated All Soul's Day,
the day of the dead. Did they see the irony in it?

In turning to a church for haven?—of praying
and taking Communion? He and Nhu must have thought
God sent men wearing uniforms from heaven,

their brass epaulettes and stars gleaming,

their ribbons of gold and blue chords braided
like the fine hairs of blonde maidens,

their boots black and polished, and their short sleeves
creased as thin as doctrines, sent them floating
to His cathedral to retrieve what He gave,

recoup Heaven's losses to restore in His home
many have dreamt of one day residing.
But I was certain when Diệm's own generals

raised him and Nhu to their feet and led them
from the long room of empty pews, the church's ceiling spiraled
to a dome of airbrushed angels and robed saints,

of jewels that pulsed with the promise of night
and with it sleep, Diệm thought
the generals were leading them to an exodus

not found in the Bible, but one mandated by Heaven,
so he believed, as the generals helped them inside the armored carrier.
And as they sat there on either side,

the doors closed, shutting out any sunlight
to allow the brothers to see each other pray
for providence long lost among the faithful.

THE FALSE FLIGHT OF ANGELS

I envy the Christ who has raised the dead,
risen even Himself from a world replete with sins.
One day when a field soldier came to me
to report the news of my son's death,
and to wait while they prepared his body for identification,
to make him presentable, the loss bearable,
I refused.

They led me through the infirmary to the back
where they kept the dead—rows and rows
of black cocoons choppered in throughout the day.
Before the coroner could point out the one,
I had already walked to Kỳ directed by my own hands
to a son I had cradled since infancy.
I unzipped the bag, bowed down and kissed him,
and from then on,
I tried to invoke Christ in Kỳ
and discovered in my attempts
that there was a harsh truth in resurrecting the dead.

*

I spent my tenure as a commandant
interrogating and torturing Việt Cộng soldiers,
and there came a sense of renewal
when seeing a man strung up by his thumbs.
The pop and give of cartilage from the weight
of suspension is like the sounds of my wives
wringing the necks of chickens and ducks,
or the breaking of sparrows in preparation for dinner;
the sounds of their cries to be cut free is comparable
to the oxen's legs buckling under the thick thud
of a sledgehammer between the eyes;
I cannot count the number of times

I had inserted slivers of bamboo beneath their fingernails;
or nailing them inside coffins with angry wingless wasps;
or the slow wiggle and turn to rend free a tooth
without the comfort of ether or morphine,
just slow enough until blood fills their mouths,
coats the backs of their throats till gargling,
even present it to them in the grips of the pliers
like some prize plucked from a Cracker Jack box.

With the already wounded,
I worked long-nosed pliers inside gashes,
maneuvered around tendons and muscles,
even reaching bone to extract bullets or shrapnel,
and I felt them seizure in the pliers I gripped.
All of this done to keep them awake in a hell heralded for me.
Like my father who once commanded the sun
to bow and show its crown, I filled the South China Sea
with the bodies of angels whose wings I had clipped
and tied behind their backs in case God gifted His angels
with the providence needed to take flight once again
to fill our nightmares with their dizzying, havoc-driven patterns.

THE BONE ORCHARD
Cambodia, 1975

Lý Loc lies on his cot,
unable to see over his stomach
as large as a bridge of rainbows.
Each time he breathes, his belly balloons taut
around his ribs like tents imprisoning wind.
When he shifts, the water crashes
against the cave of his cavity.

The patients in this bamboo hospital
watch the scarecrows wade knee-high in watery fields
to plunge rice stalks into the earth.
They roam in a straight line like cranes
standing up only to stoop to plant.
The Khmer Rouge monitor the workers weaving
around crows and magpies who pluck from the mud.

Nguyen, the armless overseer, sits in the next cot.
"They won't grow," he says when he notices
Lý Loc staring at his shoulders clean of stumps.
"I pray to Buddha; talk to the places where my arms should be."
The Khmer Rouge surround Lý Loc and point their M16s.
"If you water them daily, they will grow," Nguyen tells Lý Loc.
The men snap at Lý Loc, motion with their rifles, up, up,
and he rolls off his cot, knees bent, arms stretched
so that he falls to the floor on all fours.
The water hits ribs and lungs, and move the heart.

They lead Lý Loc outside,
past the scarecrows planting rice,
past the mocking blackbirds to the dikes
separating the mature rice fields from the young
till they arrive at a mound where Kỳ, his first born,
creates an aqueduct system out of bamboo shoots.
Stretched before them as vast as the day are fields

of milk-white bones, of faced-down ghosts;
some stare up at Heaven with empty eyes
having been proclaimed unworthy by Pol Pot
to glimpse their wrong God housed whole
behind the curtained clouds and wall of blue.
Crows rake over the bone orchard,
reaping what they can from the abundance before them.

"Come Father," Kỳ motions to Lý Loc.
One soldier says,
"They will grow if you water on a daily basis."
Kỳ inserts a bamboo into Lý Loc's navel
and water gushes from the holes Kỳ bore into the shoots.
The soldiers watch as the fields flood
and the bones begin to stir.
They uproot from the soil
and the soldiers, Kỳ, and Lý Loc
watch the water flood the fields,
washing clean the earth,
while men and women wade and weave the watery graves
to throw out their arms,
and fishing nets spin away from them
and sift the water like dust.
They haul in their nets
and caught in the mesh are bones,
hundreds of bones, thousands of bones.
The boys and girls in tiny junks untangle the bones
from the nets their parents hand them.
The adults cast fresher nets.
The Khmer Rouge lay down their weapons
and slump to their knees and pray
for the bones to become flesh once more,
for things that can fill their emptiness
and make them whole again.
The fishermen and women drag in nets and bones,
nothing but bones.

III
WHAT OF MY WIVES AND CHILDREN?

On a Bed of Salt: Van

Because of my heft, my broad back,
they send me to the salt beds of Hon Koi,
Heaven's desert of salt where the land is flat
and snow white, made whiter
by the sun's blanket of light, whiter still
by the workers dwarfed and clothed
head to toe and gloved;
their necks, mouths and noses swathed in scarves
to keep from breathing the sulfuric fumes,
eyes hidden behind mirrored sunglasses
to cut the glare of the landscape's blind white flesh.

Men and women balance baskets on poles
slung across their shoulders as they tote pieces of Heaven
across the flat land to columns only found in His sky,
tote them to construct pillars to scaffold His heaven on Earth.
Before coming here, they explained to me
the importance of layers,
how every inch of flesh must be covered.
"The hands, especially. The hands must be covered
because the salt will rough them,
eat away at the fingers to where there are holes,
to where your fingertips have no identity."

My first day mining the salt beds proves defeating—
the idea that we could extract Heaven by hand.
The guards prod me with words,
then kick me whenever I pause, or strike my back
with a bamboo pole hard enough that I can feel
their wrath's weight beneath the layers of clothes.
More than once, I find myself standing at the bottom,
thinking, *God's columns are too high to climb.*
There's too much work in building heaven from the ground up.

When the pillars prove tall enough by the end of the day,
we are sent to our respective barracks—
men separated from the women—to undress and shower any silt,
any dust, from our hair, from any exposed part of us.
I stand beneath the water, trembling not from the coldness,
but from muscles throbbing, the joints ache and sear
like fever working its way to the marrow.
My shoulders are numb, and I can barely raise my arms
to wash myself, the fingers too stiff to grip.
After getting dressed, after a bowl of rice,
we turn in for the night.

Tired to no end, I find myself outside
to men clawing to remove my clothes,
and I know they stole me
from an unwavering dream,
for I never felt the lift and carry
of my self from the barracks.
I cannot make out their faces,
only the stars above me,
the quarter moon, spying,
the weight of one man on top coming inside me.
Still I feel hands hold my arms and legs,
and I want to laugh,
for I have no strength to struggle,
or cry out in protest,
and the only sounds is of his grunting,
his wedging and wiggling to cleave me in two;
the other men breathe heavily in anticipation of their turn.
To sate their hunger while waiting,
a mouth clamps on each breast
and the men suckle greedily,
and I want to dissolve on their tongues.

When the first man finishes,
the second one climbs on me, panting

like he has the wind knocked out of him,
and still I feel nothing,
numbed to their groping and thrusting,
their wet kisses, the constant kneading and shackling
of my limbs with hands roughed by salt,
hands erased of their names,
and I want to take them all,
but I am too exhausted to even speak,
too exhausted to fight off sleep,
fight off the salt they failed to wash off
burn every part of my body
they touch and kiss
as though they learn my name
in this new place, this burning Heaven.

PROPAGANDA: THE REEDUCATION OF YÊN

What they say is a promise I can hold in my hands
like the locusts I used to pluck off lily pads and kept
for my own enjoyment as a little girl on the Perfume River.
For days, weeks even, they become comfortable enough
to the heartbeat in my palms where they stay,

where they fall asleep to the grinding of their hind legs.
This is how I take their words as I study my hands,
convinced I can see the *liberty* they speak of pulsing
in the soft, smooth whiteness of my palms, see *pride*
in not being enslaved by *foreigners* any longer,

but there are only severed barbed wire-patterned lines that join
when I cup my hands, lines Mother told me meant I was free.
I stare at the lines and wonder if why our husband
taken from us, from this house, bruised and bound
for resisting the new government's practice to right his mind

of all his lustful wrongs was a step toward this *liberty?*—
a step toward being free of Lý Loc and his other wives?
They speak of the impossible task they accomplished—
defeat the West, have them fly or boat back to their countries,
emasculated and clothed in *guilt*, the new uniform

they have tailored to fit them as familiarly and naturally
as the bones they have worn since birth; sent them home
to sit with their families at dinner time to be served *shame*
and *embarrassment* as their main meal, the very things
they have a hard time cutting with silverware polished

by dutiful wives, and an even harder time swallowing
only to feel it harden before settling in their stomachs.
At night, they toss and turn, not from getting reacquainted
with beds they left behind for the war, or with their wives'
warm bodies, places where they used to fit into each other;

64

nor from the nightmares of close mortar rounds, the blasts
a constant ringing in their ears of what hell will forever
sound like, or limbs lost from sniper fire, or head traumas
that erased all memory of speech and movement,
but from waiting for *shame* and *embarrassment* to digest,

break apart, so they can pass them from their bodies
into toilet bowls or in the woods. Sometimes they soil
their sheets and blankets. They are apologetic, insisting,
It's the war, I swear. It's the war that made me this way.
It had never happened before, and it won't happen again.

Their wives strip the beds and furl wet sheets and assure
their husbands—who stand idly by in corners, pajamas soaked,
head lowered like children—that everything will be okay,
everything will return to normal again as they hide
their husbands' humiliation should their children wake

in the middle of the night for a glass of water, or the trip
to the bathroom, to ask, "What's wrong? *Who* wet the bed?"
What is hardest is not the passing of *shame* and *embarrassment*
or finding the courage to raise their heads and address
the awaiting eyes at the dinner table, but their children know,

know what their mothers discovered when being held in bed
while familiarizing themselves with each other; they know
when being hugged or while sitting in their fathers' laps
that no matter how hard they grip at what they once let go,
there is an absence of a heartbeat in their fathers' palms.

A FAIRY TALE: YÊN

When the lily pads unfurled their elephantine ears,
it was to cup heaven's incessant weeping—
God's endless crying Mother had told me,
the only time of year He let loose sorrow upon the Earth.
That is how I remember my future husband
who came for me from a place of grieving
to our hut elevated in the middle of Sông Hương in 1963.*

Every morning, Father set out
in the rubber-patched boat he piloted
close to surrounding mountains in search of food.
During the monsoon season, his search brought him
and the other fathers inside caves
where they turned off their lanterns
and guided themselves through darkness
by distinguishing the creatures' echoes from their real sounds,
gauging the vicinity of the tail- or fin-whipped splashes,
steered themselves to the coolness the cave's walls gave off
and applied their form of Braille in reading the cracks.
Father wormed his fingers inside fissures
to extract fish, coiled eels, snails,
and higher up he would find crickets, grasshoppers,
and snakes seeking dryness.
Every day he came out of the caves
with a creel full for Mother to prepare for dinner.

One evening, Father brought forth from the cracks
his pan-shallow boat weighed down
with caged chickens covered with tarps,
baskets of pears and mangoes and lichees,
a barrel of rice, a drum of lamp oil, and rolls of silk fabric.
Flanked aside him men paddled two canoes:
one carried a pile of palm fronds

---

*Perfume River

66

and freshly hacked vines thick as ropes,
the other a tall man in uniform, sheltered
beneath an umbrella held by his Chinaman.

The boats went underneath our hut
where the men tied the caged chickens to the rafters
and the other group unloaded what would be my dowry;
the other men scaled our roof and removed old palm fronds.
They affixed the new ones and tied the vines in place.
As the Chinaman climbed the ladder first with one hand,
he held out the umbrella for Father and the uniformed man
to ascend inside our home.
With the table already set, Mother motioned
with her hands, arched eyebrows, and the jut of her chin
as to the order of the dish to be served.
As I dished out grilled mudfish with their tiny teeth removed,
frog legs, lotus buds in sesame oil and rice,
the uniformed man thanked me each time
but I simply bowed as Mother instructed me.

I studied the uniformed man,
noticed the flit of gray around his temples.
The quiet way he sipped Saki made me think
this was how he would be with me on our first night.
He would handle me with the same patience
he used in maneuvering chopsticks to pluck
the tender white meat of steamed fish,
to grope rice, the savored way he chewed lotus buds.

His two previous Tuesday wives had died,
one during childbirth, the other from tuberculosis,
and he was here for a younger replacement,
someone who would stave off grieving.
I imagined these late Tuesday wives,
the first crying out to Heaven
for having to bear a child not ready for birth,

the second one drowning in blood her lungs could not hold,
and he had been at their sides comforting them,
promising them better if they lived through this.

He slumped forward at one point
the same way, I assumed, he had been made tiny
by waiting to hear the crying of his child
or the silence of his wife's coughing.
He looked small the way a boy's shoulders slouch,
and I did two things I had been instructed not to do:
I placed my hand on him, smoothed it along the width
of his shoulders and told him,
"For you, I will live for a long time,
and you will not have to grieve anymore."

*

That night, I went to sleep to the recollection of his slow descent
            down the ladder into the boat
            and his servant draped a raincoat over him.
That night, I watched as he and his servant rowed back
            to where they came from, watched them disappear
            behind God's curtain of weeping.
That night, Mother nestled her cheek against silk I could only imagine
            she once felt as a child in some market,
            some street of her forgotten youth.
That night, as I twirled the jade ring he left me, for the first time
            during any monsoon season that I could remember,
            I slept on a dry, warm floor.
That night, I fell asleep to the sounds of caged chickens beneath me,
            huddled in feathered warmth,
            clucking in their twitched, sweet sleep.

GHOST STORIES: ÁI

Lý Loc's Friday wife resorts to the world's oldest profession.
                                        —for Robert Olen Butler

I.

One customer reminds me of my husband,
the way he removes articles of clothing
in the order he will dress himself:
the diligence in aligning the creases
of his slacks to keep them intact,
the way he folds the sleeves over the chest
before folding the midsection.
He sets his boxers over pants and shirt,
then rests the cap with its glossy visor
and insignias of rank atop his pile of clothes.

Unlike the others, he sits on the bed
to watch me undress. Sometimes,
he insists on undressing me himself.
In doing so,
he cups me from behind after removing my bra,
smells the nape of my neck as he takes the time
he is willing to pay extra for
to kiss behind my ears, along my thin shoulders,
cinches his arms around me,
afraid I will turn into an apparition in his hands.

II.

He confessed once that I reminded him of his late wife,
the one murdered while he was in the tunnels planning attacks
against the Americans, against Vietnamese officers like my husband.
He said she was thin-boned, that he delighted in the frown formed from reading,
the length between each breath when she slept,
or the languid way she backstroked the Mekong.
When he had surfaced to recoup for fresh air

69

and to commit to memory what sunlight felt like on his skin,
his commanding officer had told him. If he wanted,
he could go to the temple where she had been cremated
to mourn and pray. He had told his commander
he would forego the temple, had told him
what he knew his commander had wanted to hear:
their cause was far more important.

He had decided to set aside sorrow for when the war was over.
That first day he returned to the hole he would crawl inside and remain
for several months saddened him more than her death
because he understood the emptiness of no one to return to
when he would emerge from underground.
Though darkness swallowed him,
he heard his heart echoing the walls,
convinced it was beating through the layers of dirt and roots
and red clay so that if the living were to place their ears to the ground,
hear the *thump-thump, thump-thump,* they would swear
it was the Earth's heart in constant turmoil and sorrow.

III.

He is punctual. Lately, the times spent together are filled with talks.
Some days neither one of us gets undressed,
yet he leaves money among other things—

> a tin of tea leaves, a pouch of betel nuts I give to the other women,
> sesame seed candy molded by syrup, bouquets of longans and rambutans
> bought from vendors, an ivory comb to keep my long black hair coiled in a bun,
> a jade figurine of Buddha, a cigarette case refilled with confiscated Salems
> and Lucky Strikes, a Zippo with my name engraved: *Ái.*

More and more he stays late, even helps me make dinner,
says how food made underground was unbearable.
"Once above ground, once we won the war,
I never appreciated food as I had before."

Like the way he undresses me,
he is meticulous in paring cucumbers of their green skin
to expose their white, moist flesh;
makes sure the lid is tight so wisps of steam
do not escape when cooking rice;
that fish is grilled evenly on both sides
and that *nước mắm* has a balance of salt and sugar.

He stays long enough that the men waiting outside
fall asleep at the front door or with heads leaning
against railings, or they seek other women in this building.
We eat to the sounds of men
filling other rooms with their crying and grunting,
their need to bring their women to shriek or moan,
and these sounds echo on every floor,
down every hallway and stairwell.

Some grow impatient and leave to roam the night
in search of women who remind them of someone they lost,
their memories haunting them during their waking hours.

IV.

He has moved me into his home,
a one bedroom flat, the balcony hidden
behind tall *mai* trees lining the boulevard.
In the afternoons, they bloom yellow
in close clusters along the branches,

and in the evening they close to buds, tight as fists.
By moving me in, he says, he has absolved me
of what I once was, and that people will never see sin
when they look upon me. Every morning when he leaves
to patrol the streets to enforce right thinking and action,

enforce right speech, only then do I try on his wife's

71

áo dàis in the armoire, the long sleeved gowns with slits
creating a tri-paneled dress to allow free movement of the legs.
Some are blue and silky, some cotton.
Though most are plain, some have embroidery—

pear or cherry trees white in mid bloom,
a snarling dragon, its body roiling along the length of the sleeve
down to the hemline, its outstretched gnarled claws
groping the smaller part of my back.
I take them off after filling the place with some semblance of her life

before he comes home, suspend them on wooden hangers.
One day he comes home early while I am still dressed
in one of his wife's *áo dài*, the thinnest one of muslin.
He stands in the doorway, staring across the living room,
seeing through me, seeing the ghost of the one he lost long ago,

the one whose face he conjured up
during those long months crouched
or crawling through tunnels
while his enemies, asleep in the arms of loved ones,
dreamt above him.

THE LETTER READERS

Every piece of mail coming in is read and good news is censored with black markers.

Long gone are the days my body awoke to be nourished by lunch,
to have a chapter read to me as I sipped *Fauchon* tea
and my other maid displayed hand-washed,
sun-dried dresses for me to select for the day.
Long gone are my years as Phương, Lý Loc's Thursday wife.

4 am
and the lanterns have long lit the warehouse
before the sun thought to yawn
or turn over during slumber.
The Bunsen burners let off steam
we use to loosen the flaps moistened by tongues
that sealed news of shrinking stomachs,
the need to clothe bones
and shoe the sight of calloused soles:
relief they want as immediate and easy as folding paper.

For twelve hours a day, sometimes sixteen,
we are to censor with black markers every piece
coming in and those going out
to relatives fortunate enough to have escaped
to the gray months of England,
where French is embraced in Canada, and from America
where pockets are filled with loose change for payphones,
keys to apartments and rent houses,
bus transfers to get from one city to the next
to purchase abundance in bulk
and cart it home.

For hours we sift through Polaroids
of American customs they readily embraced:
the big stuffed, oven baked birds they hover over

with carving knives in hands; children wear masks
of men who are spiders and bats
or sheets with holes cut out to utter *boo*,
costumes that require a staff or pitchfork;
still more pictures of whole families
posing before newly bought cars,
or they stand in walkways
to homes of bricks or wood or stucco,
the lawns even and edged straight
and adorned with sprinklers, or hoses lie coiled,
their homes separated by white
or chain-linked fences or hedgerows.

They send Kodachromes of lit, tinseled trees
and silver balls dangling from limbs
with shiny-wrapped boxes crowding the bases;
of children clutching baskets in search of dyed eggs
hidden beneath brushes, leaves and tall grass.
They capture happiness and the success in accessorizing homes
with rain gutters, the paint of their choosing,
flower their garden beds with colors that attracted tribes
of butterflies, hummingbirds and bumble bees;
capture their children's surprise when getting their first puppy
or kitten, or a tank filled with fish.

Some daughters send photos of themselves smiling
as they cradle their swollen bellies, and often,
they mark how many months along they are
somewhere on the white borders.
Daily, our main office is flooded with letters
accompanied by the joy our people captured on gelatin
they shook eagerly before holding them up to their faces
in anticipation of the image that would emerge.

BLIND

Eight years old and he cannot tell his colors
the way we know to separate the pale grains of rice
from the matured dark ones. I know he will not survive
in a world that relies on colors to discriminate.
Three pages and all my government allows me
is that my grandson is an illiterate who sees hues
but does not understand their shades in meaning.

If they'd let me,
I'd teach him to read colors:
the purple marks mapping
the mended bones of my body;
the green that lives inside my lungs
and cripples my body to thinning;
the red that should river within
rather than flow outside my flesh;
the yellow that throws back the night,
stands up in the East,
walks the sky for half a day
before bedding down in the West;
and blue's burden of holding heaven in place.

THE FISHERMAN'S WIFE

Mai, Lý Loc's Monday wife

I am given to a fisherman
who sets sail just as the night begins to pale
and invite morning, and he returns
when the night is the same shade.
Each night I try to distinguish the glow
of his lanterns, the true light
of my new husband among the hundreds
who come in from the South China Sea.
But I am unable to tell him apart from the others.

While away, we wives work the prior day's catches
slicing them down their middles to extract their innards,
then pack the insides with rock salt imported from Hon Koi,
the land of acrid columns God created and cast from Heaven
to help preserve what we took from His oceans.
Some fish are as big as wives,
bigger than men even, and with these
we make sure the saw blades are sharp enough
to penetrate their thick skin,
their scales larger than thumbnails.

I never speak of Lý Loc to Tranh,
speak of how our first husband kept his hands clean,
even manicured by one of his mistresses
before touching his wives.
I try not to cringe in his handling of me every night
when we are alone, this boy of seventeen—
who looks like a man
aged by the sea gales and salt air,
the casting and hauling in of nets,
the securing of catches, and the long lonely hours left
to wander and dream on the water.
Or what he will say other than three-word sentences.

When we kiss, I breathe into him each year the ocean is old,
and his grip is tight around my hips,
tighter still when he clasps my wrists over my head
like he is working the knots out of nets
made tangled by the thrashing of a catch he needs to subdue,
a catch he does not want to let go.

A MUSEUM OF TREES

Việt, Lý Lộc's Wednesday wife, lives in Cholon, an old Chinese
district of Saigon, with her new husband.

He will not say where he gets his tubes of paint,
or the canvases he stretches taut to nail to wooden frames.
I do not want to think of how he acquires them,
what part of himself he must give up for ruining,
for I know he does not have the money,
only the allotment the government gives us:
one hundred thousand *đồngs* a month.

He spends the day on hand and knees—
a three-legged easel—combining colors
he keeps beneath the loose floorboard
in case of inspections, in case of neighbors wanting rewards.
Like the easel we offered to a neighbor to keep ourselves
out of the reeducation camp when he walked by
our door opened long enough for him to glimpse inside.

The neighbor probably exchanged it
for coffee beans he would have to grind himself,
cigarettes he would have to hand-roll;
perhaps he handed it over to a fisherman in return
for a basketful of smelt, or one large milk fish
he'd have to heft over one shoulder
down street after street before realizing
a starving country would not let him make it home.

Trang paints pictures of children holding cane poles,
their lines mirrored on the water's surface;
a boatman oaring the Mekong; farmers working striated mountains,
or doubled over in rice fields, their faces hidden
from the shadows of their sun hats;
mother with child; men at card tables,
their cigarette smoke creating clouds;

monks swathed in saffron robes, bowing before an altar;
shoulder-exposed women with downcast eyes;
and even a lone fisherman using an easel
as an improvised divinity rod to navigate his way
through the thousands of rocks in Hạ Long Bay
to set his nets and lines and hooks in hopes of finding
abundance that would forever feed him.

When done, Trang fashions wires to the frames,
and at night when everyone is asleep,
when the lanterns have all been extinguished,
we go out into the neighborhood and climb
high into the *mai* trees and bait his paintings
from their thin branches to lure passersby.
He and I know they are there, hidden during the day
when the tight-fisted buds are afire in full yellow blooms,
and at night, they close their fingers to expose the paintings,
but no one looks up anymore.

THE LAND OF DEAD CHILDREN

The dust children work the black market selling stale cigarettes,
hard chewing gum whose wrappers are as difficult to peel as wallpaper,
and sodas that no longer spit and fizz forth suds when tabs are pulled.
The packaging long empty of the promise of what was once good,
what was once desirable and quenching is all that remains.
They tote and hawk their wares on street corners,
hover over customers at soup stalls, hindering their next bite or sip of broth;
they huddle in foyers of hotels, the farthest they are allowed to enter
though vacancies are plentiful.
Every day they go out, their hair brown or red, stringy or curly,
Afros their mothers never learned to comb and treat or plait.
They go out with eyes green or black, skin freckled, tanner, noses wider,
and the only thing they have of their mothers' are the eyes.
They go out as *con lais*,* and though some are white,
they become the new niggers of Nam.
Their childhood ended having to learn the importance of pitch
to a language that requires stressed syllables.
Their faces have lost the softness essential for innocence,
and they speak with a harshness forced from wanting to be heard
over the din of the city's futile dreaming.

At night when they return home to their mothers, they eat and understand
that the silence between them is their mothers' definition for *sorry.*
The children have learned never to ask about fathers they do not remember,
fathers whose names they cannot pronounce, fathers who once cradled them to sleep
while whispering what their promised lives would be like in America.
They have learned their mothers' disappointment harnessed over their shoulders
and in their furrowed brows, the shame they inherited of how American men really are.
The mothers see the ones they once loved in their children's faces
when they watch them sleep at night, and the mothers wonder,
Are their children's dreams filled with fathers whose faces they recognize?—
do they sit on their fathers' laps while driving tractors?
The mothers wonder if in these dreams they hold their fathers' hands
on the first day of school, maybe cry when the fathers leave for work.
Or maybe they do not cry knowing their fathers will come pick them up,
eager to show them the colored construction paper cut-outs of birds with wings

---

*half breeds

80

too small to take flight, of their pet dogs, cats, and rabbits with too many whiskers,
or turkeys with each tail feather cut out and pasted on their backs;
they come running out of the schools eager to tell their fathers who they sat next to,
which friends they traded or shared their lunches with,
ready to tell them about all the things they learned that day.

The Bottom Dreamers: Tú Đức, Minh, Thanh, and Bảo

We sift the Gulf from morning till night
with nets we raise out of the water
like dreamers emerging from sleep—heavy and disoriented.
The shrimps grasp and scurry
for the right texture of their world,
and catfish swallow the unfamiliar air
and bark in protest of being caught.
We mull over market prices
from the projected weight and wonder
should we stay out on the calm waters
as we calculate how many more seasons
must we save before we own
our own restaurant in Port Arthur.
We contemplate making night runs
past Galveston deep into Trinity Bay
where we had witnessed—more often
than we cared to admit to our wives—
the parade of boats brandishing burning crosses
to ward off the Negro and Asian fishermen.

We bring in the largest loads,
the Gulf as familiar to us as the Tonkin,
but not as humid, not even green,
and like Tonkin, we know how far out to anchor.
Our radius spans as wide as God's girth
required to haul in the abundance of His gifts;
we read the tides as easily as we read
the sky's gloomy mood of winter,
the spring and summer blue that gives.
For this, they mock us whenever we dock
by drawling our syllables like violin music,
or they call their dogs to them.
We sell our loads on scales offset in their favor,
the market prices having dropped suddenly

during those hours spent on the water,
the weight of shrimps and catfish insufficient
of carrying out any dream.

Still, we make bank deposits
where it will grow into a sum large enough
to purchase the building long abandoned
on 9th Avenue and 7th Street,
convert the boarded windows,
the gutted walls and sawed off pipes
where sinks used to be,
the floor cement-gray and water-stained in places
where sun and rain filters through;
convert the place to provide for our own
who yearn once more to sit on the low-lying stools
of their family kitchens to the sounds of their mothers
and grandmothers searing fish and fowl in skillets,
broths simmering in cauldrons;
a place where those who came by boat
can converge and let loose the weight
of our language's syllables to stress our losses.
A place where we can express doubts of ever returning
to a country of kitchens filled with our mothers' knives
constantly cutting and chopping meat to the rhythm
of their humming as we waited beneath
the tables among the outstretched legs of our father
and older brothers who ate first
the choice portions of meat, fish and shrimps;
we picked up whatever scraps they dropped—
fish and chicken bones and shrimp tails we learned to grind down
to a pulp to make swallowing bearable,
dream of the day we can afford to bring Father over
to America, to this region called Texas,
and show him the restaurant we built by owning the Gulf,
that we are now big enough to get off the floor
and sit at the same table with him.

FIDÈLE

I.

Here, in Ruston, there are no synagogues;
no temples or pagodas with extended eaves
or tiled roofs and bamboo gardens, meditating ponds
with waterfalls, or monks swathed in saffron robes;
there are no gongs to punctuate each prayer
to our dead ancestors; only churches whose steeples
are wooden hands formed in prayer—a congregation
of confessed sins to be forgiven.

II.

Each evening I tend the herbs in our garden:
spear- and peppermint, lemon and purple basil—
leaves lush and waxen and ruffled as tuxedo cuffs,
Chinese chives and stalks of lemon grass
I traveled an hour to purchase in Shreveport.

Each evening, the Boudreaux's—
with their three year old son, Seth, and Myra in a stroller—
take walks with Noah, their lab, up and down McBride Road.
They smile white and wide, their skin pale.
They praise my garden and admire my progress

before speaking of the love they have for Jesus,
and they want to share His love with us. The crosses they wear
glimmer with the divine light of God. They ask if I've found Jesus.
Ask if I know what it is like to wear His shroud
and feel my sins absorbed in its fabric?

Ask, as I smudge aphids between thumb and forefinger,
if I would like to attend service? I shake my head,
tell them *no thank you*, as my husband instructed me.
Smiling, they nod and continue their walk through the cul de sac
to shake the hands of neighbors whose prophet died for their sins.

III.

They come as punctual as prayer,
baring their legs and arms as white as teeth,
the husband's well-trimmed honey-colored beard.

Their heads are adorned with halos of sunlight following them.
They extend another invitation as they stand above me
while I crouch in the garden that sustains my family.

Seth picks up an onion from my colander of harvest
and hurls it like a baseball and the proud Boudreaux's smile;
Noah lifts a leg against the lemon grass

and I grip tight the trowel: "Yes. I will go."
Their smiles take in more joy than they deserve,
their eyes glint with the prospect of witnessing,

and all hope suddenly softens when I offer them a place
at my temple in Shreveport: "I will pray to your God,
and next week you can light incense sticks,

kneel and chant prayers before Buddha to *my* dead ancestors."
With cleared throats, they mutter how nice it would be,
and Mr. Boudreaux tugs on Noah's leash.

IV.

Wrath consumes me—a word I have overheard spat forth from the faithful,
spittled from the mouths of televangelists whose arms are always outstretched
above their sculpted, unmoving hair, Bible in hand, eyes shut tight from the weight
of their rapturous words—when I stand before the uprooted onions, mints,
and the chives are strewn like straw across our front lawn,

the words *gooks* and *slopes* accompanied with *go home* spray-painted on our driveway.

My husband and I spend the morning on our knees, a bucket of warm water
and Tide between us as we bristled white suds into the black words.
All I can think of is the wrath I feel—the hope of their freckled flesh festering with boils,

of locusts ravaging God's landscape of steeples and marquees welcoming the weary and lost,
wish everlasting fires consume their cemeteries adorned with crosses

and prayerful gray gowned, marbled angels. Heat brimstones my whole body

as my husband's furrowed brow holds up the weight of the day's heat made evident by sweat.
We scrub, thinking their generosity has been long forgotten from sermons,
long burned by the southern sun and drowned by spirits. When done, there remains
McBride Road's sin hard of cleansing, hard to consider the idea of forgiveness.
The neighborhood's love is as thin as their Bible pages, their faith as tiny as the type.

We speak of what is best for our daughters, speak of the weight of His suffocating shroud,

and I spend the afternoon on the phone with Vu-An, my half-sister, who beckons us
to California to a place called Silver Lake, where there is an ocean in one direction,
the desert in the other, snow up north, and mountains all around. They live in an alcove
named Asia Minor where their kids are brown and white and loved; they grow what they want
in fenced-in gardens they are allowed to erect and amend; where Vu-An sews clothes.

"Come, Pham," Vu-An says, "where we even have a place called Little Saigon."

The Shape of Things

I. The Seamstress

José, the sweatshop owner, assigns each woman
a different color safety pin
to know how much to pay us:

Maria is orange like the plumage of Bird of Paradise
grown in her native Colombia;
Patricia is green as the desert cactuses of Arizona.

I have a job sewing blouses,
dresses, skirts, and slacks,
and I get paid per piece stitched.

I spend eight hours a day
attaching cuffs to sleeves,
collars around necklines,

joining two pant legs to form
slacks that flair at the bottom,
mend zippers to seal womanhood,

hem the length of skirts to disclose
age and promiscuity, procure promotions
and maintain modesty.

Hue, another Vietnamese woman, is black
as the sparrows her mother purchased
from marketplaces only to snap their necks

in preparation for the evening's meal;
Linda is yellow as the canaries caged
for her children's enjoyment.

I stitch buttons along one side
of blouses, create slits on the other half
by which they pass through.

When I am through, I hang
my finished product on racks, then,
I pin papered patterns of cuffs

and collars and pants, and if they part,
trace skirts and slit lines against fabric
that will clothe a person whole.

Veronica is as red as the blood of her Christ;
Clara is pink as our calluses,
and I, I am always blue.

II. A Janitor's Job

My husband cleans the college he attends.
He works long hours washing clean the blackboards
of all its Spanish and French conjugations,
its mathematical equations that search
for precise volumes to triangles and circles,
the measurement of angles.

He wipes clean the history of Hitler's reign
in Poland, Austria, France, and Germany,
of Jews emaciated, gassed, and cremated,
of Hirohito's kamikazes and the mushrooms
flowering over Nagasaki and Hiroshima;
the Great Depression and Roosevelt's New Deals for a better future;
erases the slave revolts and voting rights
right on through to *Roe v. Wade* and bra burning;
and he continues, passing felt over draft numbers
and conscientious objectors,
and the U.S.'s fallacies of the domino theory

in South East Asia, and I think of you falling to a new regime;
I think of you starving in a country that promised hope.

He works his hours one class to the next,
erasing what professors wrote from rote of years
spent doubled over books spread before them
and read beneath dim lit lamps,
years of clenching their hands of cramps
crimped from extensive note-taking,
and reminded themselves to straighten
their backs free of stiffening.

When his shift is through,
he sits in the very same classrooms the next day,
witnessing history
chalked on a clean black slate.

III. The Care Package

The box does not hold everything
I want to give you.
There is a bottle of aspirin, 200 count,
for any pain you suffer,
canned lichees in heavy syrup,
walnuts, pecans, and almonds,
a carton of Salems for mornings on the porch
and after dinners,
and dress shirts of yellow,
blue, white, and tan,
their sleeves pinned behind them,
their collars creased and stiff,
buttoned from top to bottom,
their torsos folded in half
and wrapped in crinkled cellophane.

And here. Here, enclosed, are Polaroid's

of your grandson, Long-Vanh.
See how his wrists have grown
beyond the cuffs of his shirts,
how the hem of his pants
expose his thin ankles.
See how he grows,
tall and healthy in America.

YÊN'S INTERLUDE

Each second of sunlight is the wrong note
held too long upon my body.
Bound to this tree for the third day,
ants have composed red rashes upon my flesh,
and the ropes have numbed my wrists and ankles,
making it difficult to keep time.

The rest finally comes when they bring Yên,
my youngest wife, to the camp,
and I am ashamed to have her see me this way—
put aside, reeking of urine, skin crawling with ants and flies.
I think she is here to claim me,
to tell the escorting officer
that she is to take me home to rejoin the other wives
so I can hear them harmonize in the kitchen,
to collaborate in our beds.

Yên only stares at me, and it is when she blinks
I notice she is off key as my wife,
for she looks like the man standing next to her:
her hair is short like a boy's.
Her chest is flat in the uniform she wears,
her pants are rolled up to expose her thin ankles,
and my fingers strain to play her body once more.

I part my lips to speak,
but my tongue betrays me in forming the right melody
that will loosen her jaw.
How she has turned in this moment—
to fall out of love with the man who sang to her
without her opening that door to her throat for a request.

She moves toward me,
hands behind her back,

an idle metronome.
When she is close enough, I expect one hand
to come from behind her back to conduct a slap,
or to set it upon my cheek, assure me everything will be okay.
She looks up at me from beneath her pith helmet.
Though her lips part,
no song sung nor hummed would ever come from her.
She is working her tongue in a circle,
and before I realize she has been working
and worrying free a wad of spit,
it is in my face.

I watch as she warms up and works her tongue,
again,
certain she will practice this new song
until she finds the exact pitch
to strike that right note.

Epilogue

You can kill ten of my men for every one I kill of yours. But even at those odds, you will lose and I will win.

—Hồ Chí Minh

THE STARVING CITY: NHA TRANG '75

The rice fields are oceans of green blades
surging beneath the winds,
and the fields compose the receding sounds of the sea.

Beyond the Central Highland Mountains,
the South China Sea stretches away from Phương Trần Phú
cluttered with idle motorbikes starving for petrol,
rickshaws' pedals like palms thrust out for fares.
The bar is absent of American soldiers
roaming the nights for taps which never stopped flowing
--here soldiers found God in the sticky tar-balls
heated and twirled from the ends of sticks
and plunged inside the navels of clay cherubs
from which they drew breath for sleep;
those absent from the bar found rooms above guarded by St. Peter.
For the right amount of *đồngs*, he admitted the lost
to be housed in His many rooms filled with angels
shedding thigh-length dresses or mini-skirts
and go-go boots to expose skin as white
and unblemished as clouds. Some soldiers said
it was like watching angels detach their wings
to expose flesh, so heavenly and virginal.

Now, people mill about with pockets
lined with lint and filled with empty hands.
Children suck dirt off their thumbs,
from between fingers, and their bellies swell with dreams
of fowl and pork, of noodles and rice, of thin-shelled lichees:
pink pearls of sweet flesh and hard-seeded centers.
St. Peter has cast the angels from the abundant, empty rooms
to roam Phương Trần Phú to bring the lost to the fold.
They stand on the corners: their haggard hair hides
their sleep deprived faces, their long sleeves sheave
the purpled, punctured marks along their blade-like arms,

and their white skirts and boots, gowns and stockings are now dirtied
as they pine for men who mumbled prayers and whimpered confessions
while in the arms of their favorite angel.

Yet the angels still walk past businesses that open for show,
and people barter tangerine peels,
potato vines, round shaped, freckled pears,
pregnant strands of kelp, brown-leafed morning glories
and mangoes bruised from thumbing; they barter
these items for bottles of fermented scorpions and geckos
and plum wines for ducks, chickens and dogs,
for fish whose lips part for air
only to discover the world outside their oceans
is empty of the promise of breathing.

Acknowledgments

In the Spring of 2010, Dean Don Kaczvinsky asked if I wanted the visiting poet to come and speak to my creative writing class since he would be doing a reading later that evening. I said, "Sure. Why not?" Darrell Bourque spoke to my class, and afterwards he asked me what I wrote. I told him fiction, and he wondered if I wrote poetry. I mentioned I had started on a group of poems in 2002 after my first trip back to Vietnam, and he said he would like to read them. I explained to him that there were nine unfinished poems about my grandfather who had seven wives and twenty-seven children. "They're unfinished," I reiterated, "and they've just been sitting there for these eight years." He insisted I send them to him, which I did.

Within two days he e-mailed me and encouraged me to finish them, and to write however many more poems it would take to tell my grandfather's story, and not just his, but his wives', his children's, and even mine. "His story needs to be heard. It needs to be out there. His story is important to us all," was how Mr. Bourque put it. It is because of him these poems were completed during the span of the next two summers. Because of him, I renewed my love for writing and my roots, and my grandfather, his wives, and children can live again in print.

Special thanks goes out to Caleb Elkins and Heather Castille, former students who called me and Dr. John Martin one day and asked if we would like to be a part of their poetry workshop that summer of 2010, which was something I needed in order to finish *The Land Baron's Sun*. So I want to thank Caleb, Heather, John, April Honaker, Drs. Kenneth and Dorothy Robbins, and Dr. Nicole de Fee for the rigorous, demanding but enjoyable workshops which also consisted of homemade dinners, wine, and invaluable critiques and company I so immersed myself into every Wednesday night. You are all very much appreciated.

I want to thank Jon Tribble and his wonderful wife, Allison Joseph, for publishing "Vacation," "Providence," and "The Starving City" in *Crab Orchard Review* 16.1 (2011); Matthew Silverman and Lenore Weiss for publishing "A Museum of Trees," "Propaganda: The Reeducation of Yên," "View from the Veranda: An Elegy for Chan," and "Grasping" in *Blue Lyra Review* 2.3 (2013); Jessica Pitchford for selecting "The Fisherman's Wife" for *Pembroke Magazine* 45; Ralph Adamo for publishing "The Shape of Things" in the *Xavier Review* 32 1/2 (2012), and Paul Lai who chose "The Bone Orchard" for publication in *Kartika Review* 11.1 (2011).

I am very grateful to the members of the Louisiana Board of Regents for awarding me the ATLAS grant which afforded me time off to work on this book as well as *The Beautiful Ones Are Not yet Born*. This grant, however, would never have been possible if it were not for the help, encouragement, and insistence by Dr. Bill Willoughby who helped put together the grant and walked me through each step until completion. Though a meticulous and demanding process, I want to thank him for his time and patience.

I am also grateful to James D. Wilson Jr. of the Center for Louisiana Studies and Associate Director of the University of Louisiana at Lafayette Press for selecting the book and for working with me, and Mary Karnath Duhé and Michael Martin for their keen editing and critiques.

Thanks to Robert Olen Butler for teaching me the one important element needed in any genre of writing. I would not have achieved as much as I have if it were not for that phone call in the spring of 1996, asking if I wanted to come out to Lake Charles for three years. One of the best decisions artistically and academically that I had ever made.

To my wife, Robyn, who allowed me to pursue my endeavors as a poet every Wednesday night, and when I had trouble with a poem, she was very useful in pinpointing the problems. She was very much a helpful reader, even offering "Repletion" as a title.

To my mother, Ngoc Thi, for all those stories about my grandfather, and finally to Lý Loc whose only memory I have of him is that he gave me his sugarcane when I finished all of mine.